AF226063

Love speaks
for
Romance,

Love speaks
more for
Compassion.
- Quoted

Credit goes to
poet LuCxeed,
and the team of designers,
photographers, cartoonists,
and editors at the publisher: D'Moon

ISBN: 978-1-933187-56-3

Your feedback is most welcome ~
publisher@worldculturepictorial.com

LuCxeed
collection 1.
Selected LuCxeed Poems
Train of Morrow
1
poetry
song lyrics
photo & art
philosophy
d'moon books

Contents

Quote from introduced poem

Contents

"Deep into midnight, cry
in soundless silence. Sky
is weeping, tears falling so slow
frozen into crystal snow
to quiet down the around
in dark, laying mourning white"

Train of Morrow

"(No noise, be silent)
My step is cautioned,
Not to intrude,
Not to disturb,
the forever grand,
stately mood
of each
redwood."

Contents

"I wonder
where you are?
my other half
with my other half soul"

Quote in art Calligraphy &
introduced poem title   28 - 29

"Is Past a past
or a ghost?
Or, as birthmark, a halo
on Train of Morrow.
Mind of Time, haunted,
disturbed, confused,
cannot think, nor rest."

Contents

"Little spots, round and shallow,
Scatter over the snow.
Footprints loyally follow
The soulful, tiny shadow."

Train of Morrow

"Quietness is emotionless.
Emptiness is wordless.
Memory is restless."

Contents

"Sickness knocks
winter into summer,
Life almost out of life,
into an insentient sickbed,
into depressive distress,
into secret regret."

"Future spells uncertainty.
What should I do?
...
The scale quivers.
Reason runs out of Sense."

Contents

"Emotion takes off into storm -
The ocean of clouds is in gloom,

mingling Future and Past,
twisting Love and Lust,
meandering Affection's trek,
melting Rationale's legs."

"Dream of Glory -
     unhand me! Leave me be!
Mercy!
     My Lord of Fame."

Contents

"Day sneaks around.
Night won't shut down.
Clock arms lazily crawl.
Each hour is dreadfully long.
Sickbed locks me as a cell in hell."

"Have we ever met
or not acquainted yet
Where'll our fate be led
Who's spinning the thread"

Contents

"I'll be gone to the battlefield
Don't wait for me long, my darling
Just hand me our engagement ring
Remember me yet you're free"

"She said with a gaze
Into the distance
"I want to be a bird
at my next birth."
Her gaze is fixed
at the edge of the earth."

Contents

"Love's footsteps,
scattered along the pageless B.C.,
between the lines of modern times,
into future history
      dotted on silicon chips"

(Thank you for being here!)

Quote a poem
to introduce
the poem

in art calligraphy
Q

quote "weeping sky"
to introduce the poem

Deep into midnight, cry
in soundless silence. Sky
is weeping,
tears falling so slow
frozen
into crystal snow
to quiet down
the around
in dark, laying
mourning white

(No noise, be silent)
My step is cautioned
Not to intrude,
Not to disturb,
the forever grand,
stately mood
of each
redwood.

quote "half soul's hope"
to introduce the poem

I wonder
where you are?
my other half
with my other half soul

Is Past a past
or a ghost?
Or, as birthmark, a halo
on Train of Morrow.
Mind of Time, haunted,
disturbed, confused,
cannot think, nor rest.

29

A Little spots,
round and shallow,
Scatter over the snow.
Footprints loyally follow
The soulful, tiny shadow.

uietness is emotionless.
Emptiness is wordless.
Memory is restless.

31

quote "secret regret"
to introduce the poem

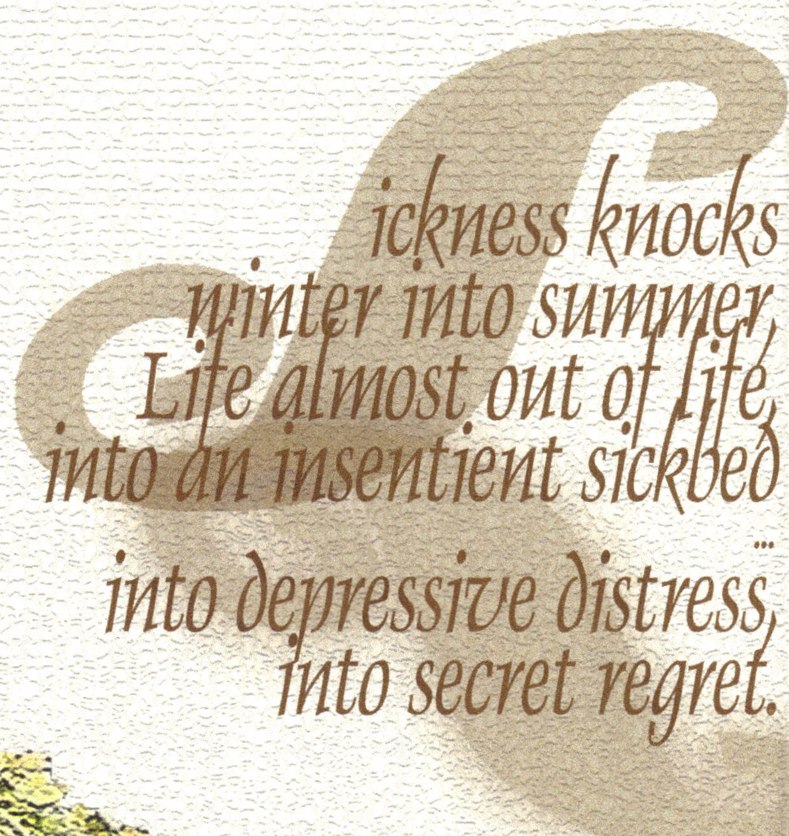
Sickness knocks
winter into summer,
Life almost out of life,
into an insentient sickbed
...
into depressive distress,
into secret regret.

Future
spells uncertainty.
What should I do?
...
The scale
quivers.
Reason
runs
out of Sense.

quote "so long"
to introduce the poem

Emotion takes off into storm –
The ocean of clouds is in gloom..

...

mingling Future and Past,
twisting Love and Lust,
meandering Affection's trek,
melting Rationale's legs.

Dream of Glory —
unhand me!
Leave me be!
Mercy!
My Lord of Fame.

quote "secret regret"
to introduce the poem

Day sneaks around.
Night won't shut down.
Clock arms lazily crawl.
Each hour
is dreadfully long.
Sickbed locks me
as a cell in hell.

quote "have we ever met"
to introduce the poem

Have
we ever met
or not acquainted yet
Who's
spinning the thread
Where'll our fate be led

37

quote "Soldier's Engagement Ring"
to introduce the poem

I'll be gone
to the battlefield
Don't wait for me long,
my darling
Just hand me
our engagement ring
Remember me
yet you're free

She
said with a gaze
Into the distance
"I want to be a bird
at my next birth."
Her gaze is fixed
at the edge of the earth.

Love's footsteps,
scattered
along the pageless B.C.,
between the
lines of modern times,
into future history
dotted on silicon chips

Thank
you
for being
here!

POEM

@ poetry in gallery®
poem in art

Weeping Sky

Deep into midnight, cry
in soundless silence. sky
is weeping, tears falling so slow
frozen into crystal snow
to quiet down the around
in dark, laying mourning white

Unyielding. Eyes, half shut
speak oceans of unspoken
comprehended
by hands in hands
soaked in streaming tears

Weeping Sky

Time stolen. Heart, broken
whispers into departing
          Dearest's ears
"...can you hear me? remember
my love, uncompromising,
             will forever
walk beside you...anywhere...
                    ever..."

        "Hear ya -" outside
muffled echoes of broken heart,
                    crying
tears falling from far above,
                  so slow
frozen into crystal snow
Darkness solemnly wears
            mourning white
Sky weeping...deep midnight

Visit my Confidant

A redwood, ever-lived,
skyward, gallant,
in a forest,
is my confidant.
A dwelling
of naturehood,
magnificent,
(not a bit arrogant)
swelling with
noble livelihood.

Visit My Confidant

(No noise, be silent)
My step is cautioned,
Not to intrude,
Not to disturb,
the forever grand,
stately mood
of each
redwood.

Seated at the foot
of the ancient giant,
my Calm Confidant,
(deep breath,
much confident)
"With all due respect,
I sincerely ask...
I appreciate you're patient..."
So much to talk...
Where to start?

LuCxeed Poem

Visit My Confidant

My lovely hometown,
childhood,
or adventurous
adulthood,
taken in by grandeur of
redwoods
my eyes closed... my heartland
lit up by one word,
"understood" -
it must come
from my Redwood
Confidant.

LuСхеед Роеm

Half Soul's Hope

I wonder
were we separated
were we created
into two
where are you
my other half
with my other half soul

LuCxeed Poem

I wonder
where you are
dwelling in a mountain
voyaging the ocean
Are you lonesome
without me
as I am without you

I wonder
where you are
Clouds gather
Valley echoes thunder
Appetence in silence
Ground takes in raindrops
heavy with a half soul's hopes

Half Soul's Hope

I wonder
where you are
Clouds scatter
Grass is greener
The sky bluer
Breeze brings no sign
Tree I lean on is still. Leaves sigh

I wonder
where you are
my other half
with my other half soul
Evening stars twinkle
One must have a buckled inkle
and hint an inkling from

you to me
I to you

LuСхeeд Poem

Train of Morrow

Is Past a past
or a ghost?
Or, as birthmark, a halo
on Train of Morrow.
Mind of Time, haunted,
disturbed, confused,
cannot think, nor rest.

LuCxeed Poem

Does Past not exist,
yet hold shackles,
or, like jesting shadow
on Train of Morrow?
Mind of Time, chained,
frustrated, wrangle
to be free, to go.

Is Past dead, a ghost
reshaping in forms,
flitting around
as well on Train of Morrow?
Everything, flying, out of windows,
Mind of Time, weakened,
hanging on, hanging on.

Train of Morrow

Is Past, as birthmark, a halo
over the head, also
boarding on
Train of Morrow?
"Don't fall off", warned
by train's speed, and rhythm,
Mind of Time, hanging on.

Mind of Time, impossible to
straighten out:
"not my fault,
logic goes wrong",
in the smoke of, the whistle of,
Train of Morrow,
hanging on, hanging on...

LuCxeed Poem

Giant White
Mirrors moonlight,
Encircled by Frontier of Blue.
Air is crystal.
        Sound sealed by icy glue.

Little spots, round and shallow,
Scatter over the snow.
Footprints loyally follow
The soulful, tiny shadow.

"You can see him home, right?"
Moon blinked at Giant White –
"Into quite a distance, far and away."
Frontier of Blue, starry. Stars
        lightly sway.

LuCxeed Poem

Night guards footprints
in speechless beauty.
Nature consoles the shadow
with unbesmirched purity.

A Little Sad Shadow

"My Whiteness leads you nowhere,
    my dear fellow.
Moonlight's willing to visit those
    you want to say hello."

Quiet Moon enshrouded
    by bright moonlight,
Underneath is Giant White,
Matted by Frontier of Blue.
Air is crystal. Sound
    sealed by icy glue.

More little spots,
    round and shallow,
Scatter over
    the sympathetic snow.
More footprints follow
The little sad shadow.

LuCxeeд Poem

A Cottage

A nest, a cottage with ridged
roof, fringed edge,
once a crowded lodge,

lost its bustling, flighty,
      cheery chirps;
lost darting dances in chirrups,
lost joyful tears
      in countless hugs.

A once-crowded nest
waves goodbye
to each fledgling taking flight

LuCxeed Poem

as each little bird
fetches a full plumage, girded
with courage to soar, to glide,

watched by the dutiful parent,
staying behind in good stead,
a pioneer who erected the nest,

64

once filled with
bustling, flighty, cheery chirps,
with darting dances in chirrups.

Quietness is emotionless.
Emptiness is wordless.
Memory is restless.

"You're free now
to fledge your freedom,
to feather wings of your dream."

Caring, comforting voice
            of the cottage,
a once-happily-crowded nest
            with ridged
roof, standing in raindrops —
            with fringed edge.

Secret Regret

Sitting on Sickbed,
Life is numb as eyes
fix on the aloof calendar -
It highlights July,
mid-summer.
Why?
Feel as cold as in December!

How ruthless -
at a gust of feeble breeze,
Life sneezes
and coughs breathlessly
as if an old man, sick
in the howling blast
with winter in the chest.

Soup, tasteless.
Food, flavorless.
Mixed with fruits
of precise science,
flawless pills
in artificial hues -
red, orange, blue.

"Swallow them
spoon by spoon,"
nurses persistently
insist -
"no compromise."
As well, no choice.
Deprived of freedom,
Life is pallid and wan.
Dumb.

LuCxeed Poem

Sickness knocks
winter into summer,
Life almost out of life,
into an insentient sickbed,
into bullying bills,
into depressive distress,
into secret regret.

Sickbed is blind to
time's fraud.
Day sneaks around.
Night won't shut down.
Clock arms lazily crawl.
Each hour is dreadfully long.
Sickbed locks me
          as a cell in hell.

Secret Regret

One month.
Three months.
Wealth
has run away with Health,
forsaken Life
to be threatened
by Death.

Sickness knocks
winter into summer,
Life almost out of life,
into sickbed for the weak,
for the sick, for the lost,
sickbed locks me
          as a cell in hell.

LuCxeed Poem

Frustrated.
Sick of Sickbed.
Life rises, escapes
into the forest,
into sunlit spots,
onto a tree's
huge roots,

collapses
upon Nature's chest,
weeps in deep regret.
Quests in earnest –
Health,
life of Life,
please––, come back–––

LuCxeed Poem

Mercy! My Lord of Fame

Mercy! My Lord of Fame

One of many
a thousand-mile journey
acquaints me with a lady
from my home county.

Braggingly chancy.
If calling it chance.

A willowy silhouette drifts
into a bachelor's sight
The day I'm boarding
for a far-away continent.

Meant to be?
Or merely coincident?
Ridiculous. Yet content.

LuCxeed Poem

Seconds after I mock myself
as a holed-up murky frog,
a fortune reading
mimics my thought.

What a dolt's joke!
Blockhead!

Lustrous tresses, tender fingers
tug at strings of my heart;
the more we chat,
the more I'm enchanted.
Indeed. Indeed.

Is she an innocent soul?
Or, am I a fool?

Mercy! My Lord of Fame

Songs for her skip
out of my voice,
breaking deep,
depressive ice.

Passion asks for patience.
My lonely hut
shrugs off silence.

Converse much
about childhood, livelihood,
about evolution of everything,
and of statehood.

Witty. Talented.
Briskly too good.

LuCxeed Poem

Yet, she is true, indeed true.
Future spells uncertainty.
What should I do?

Decisively indecisive.
Hopeless hope.

A dainty silhouette
with an untainted soul
on one hand.
Treasure of Fortune,
Fame of Name,
on the other.

Mercy! My Lord of Fame

The scale quivers.
Reason runs out of Sense.

Whoops, Fame sweeps
me off my feet to depart.
Ambition rolls over
the love of Heart.

Rethink about it – any regrets?
Forget about it. Which is what?

A lady brings
sunshine into my life.
Don't let her go.
Dream of Glory –
unhand me! Leave me be!

Mercy!
My Lord of Fame.

Morning Dew

enclosed in outer petals
and
sepals is fragile gold and pink
amidst the spraying mist
morning dews
shining fragile gold and pink
skipping from leaves to sepals
rolling up
hanging on
mounting up
to enlarge the clear crystal
spherical palace

Morning Dew

wrapping in tree
leaves, green
and own fragile gold and pink
more and more
bigger and bigger
shivering and reshaping
in a gentle blow of wind
inside the dew drop
reaching almost perfect shape
is a whole life

"Slow down, hold on
Before I finish...
The perfect mystique
Soon be gone"

LuCxeed Poem
"I want to be a Bird"

"I want to be a bird
at my next birth,"

She said with a gaze
into the clouds.

"With wings into the winds,
so light to fly."

She said with a gaze
into skies.

"So much they can see.
Merely they are free."

"I want to be a bird"

She said with a gaze
into the distance

"I want to be a bird
at my next birth."

Her gaze is fixed
at the edge of the earth.

You're heard, Friend.
Joy of chat quietly quit in haze.

Holding more than words said,
her eyes in deep gaze.

Empty Bottle

If lined up,
it must be a long line
of shuffled empty
bottles of beer, of wine,
of schnapps, of tequila,
of scotch, of vodka,
though few were
guzzled with pride.

My wife had threatened
to, and did, abandon me.
My son had yelled
to, and did, leave me.
"Am I an empty soul?"
Damn it!
"Am I an empty bottle?"
Damn it!

Empty Bottle

Glasses glitter,
Lights dim.
Warm is the bar,
Intense is the Rum.
Construction's tough,
with lurking harm.
Loneliness is such a pain.
Unbroken doom.

Had empty bottles
not buried an empty
soul, there
must be my burned hopes,
unshed tears
inside the empty bottle.
Whirl. swirl.

Have we ever met?

Have we ever met
or not acquainted yet
Can I forget I've felt
I know you as I do myself

Refined, solid
and upstanding
Kind, candid
and understanding

LuCxeed Poem

Eyes meet eyes,
    like a spring stream
joining another
    gentle spring stream
Spirit touches spirit.
    Intensity beams
Voiceless soul teems
    with sunlit charm

Have we ever met?

Have we ever met
or not acquainted yet
where'll our fate be led
Who's spinning the thread

Eyes meet eyes, charmed
Intensity beams
Spirit touches spirit
Deep. Genteel. Sunlit

Have we ever met
or not acquainted yet
Can I forget I've felt
I know you as I do myself

You must be
as young
as my heart
will ever be

Soldier's Engagement Ring

Soldier's Engagement Ring

I'll be gone to the battlefield
Don't cry, my darling
Just return to me
      our engagement ring

I'll be gone to the battlefield
Don't wait for me long, my darling
Just hand me our engagement ring

Remember me yet you're free
I'll ever hold the pair of rings
To my heart as I'm holding
      you now, my darling

I'll be gone to the battlefield
Don't cry. Don't cry, my darling
Just return to me
      our engagement ring

Emotion takes off into storm,
no thought to be pored on.
She said so long –
"Love goes wrong..."

Emotion takes off into storm,
no thought to be pored on.
He said so long –
"Love is gone..."

So Long

Emotion takes off into storm,
The ocean of clouds
is in gloom.
They parted –
"Why waste time on
one for long..."

Emotion takes off into storm,
Burned
is Bridge for Wisdom
to walk on.
They parted –
"...too much, too long..."

she said so long –
"Love goes wrong..."
He said so long –
"Love is gone..."

They parted
before long;
We parted
due to too long.

Who said that
nothing is sad?
Unless nothing is true in what
they once had,
in what we once had.

So Long

Emotion takes off
into storm –
no thought to be pored on;
no common ground to stand on.
The ocean of clouds is in gloom,

mingling Future and Past,
twisting Love and Lust,
meandering Affection's trek,
melting Rationale's legs.

So long is said.
Sad to, or not to, say so long.
Any unburned bridge
for Wisdom to walk on?

LuCxeed Poem

I search for Love's footsteps,
as many do,
scattered along the pageless B.C.,
between the lines of modern times,
into future history
dotted on silicon chips,
stretching in an infinite space.

Love's Footsteps

I listen to Love's footsteps,
as many do,
to hear where it descends,
      it dances, it glees;
when it halts, it sobs,
      it angers, it flees.
Incurably innocent.
      Love quests for oneness,
solicitude, not for the loveless,
      nor for less.

I follow Love's footsteps, as
a slight boat in dark
      does a lighthouse,
to find an ideal place to
      create a warm palace
of Truth, of Simplicity, of Beauty.
Where is the oasis?
"Where I meet Wisdom,"
      Love whispers.

www.ingramcontent.com/pod-product-compliance
Lightning Source LLC
Chambersburg PA
CBHW040722070726
47637CB00018B/15